THE TRUE LIFE OF AN APOSTLE

THE TRUE LIFE OF AN APOSTLE

Apostle
Dr. Valerie Jackson
Foreword By: Dr.Rickardo Bodden

Published by
Daughters of Distinction LLC

The True Life of an Apostle
Published by Daughters of Distinction LLC
Copyright ©2021 by Dr. Valerie Jackson

Printed in the United States of America

Unless otherwise noted, all Scripture quotations are taken from the Holy Bible, New King James Version.

Scripture quotations marked NKJV are from the New King James Version, Copyright ©1982 by Thomas Nelson, a division of HarperCollins Christian Publishing, Inc.

End-of-verse references and book introductions copyright © 2006 by Thomas Nelson. All rights reserved.

DEDICATION

I dedicate this book to my late parents: John and Annie Parrott, who sacrificed everything to raise, mold and shape me into the Godly woman I am today, my children: Devone, Brittney, Jordan and Samuel, my siblings: Leon, Diane and Annett, my Made In His Image Church Family and lastly, but not least my best friend of 22 years, my husband: Lynn Jackson, who continuously cheers me on in every endeavor and makes sure I do not give up.

REVIEW

It has been a long time coming for such a penning of a profound manual to shift the Office of The Apostle back to its intended purpose of purity and Apostolic Authority. The timing of The True Life of An Apostle, is being birthed at a time when the whole Earth is experiencing what we know it to be as a "RESET". For the past thirty plus years, we have seen a tainting of the Office of the Apostle that has produced a lustful stench in the Kingdom of God. We have seen many make this Office to be about money, fancy clothes, shoes and entourages. This type of false glamorous presentation has caused many to step into this office either prematurely or unaffirmed by GOD, unfilled without the leading of Holy Spirit, powerless, wounded and not healed. We have seen and experienced the tragic error of man's choice instead of GOD's.

I reread this book about four times before writing this review. Every time I went to reread sections of this book Holy Spirit revealed so much more than the other times, which caused me to appreciate the birthing process of servanthood even more. Apostle Dr. Jackson imparts Godly wisdom and knowledge on what to expect through the various stages of emerging and seasoned leadership. Holy Spirit uses her to explain and redefine what the Office of the Apostle is and to know what your Sphere of Influence is within the call of the Apostleship. She is always ready to teach and adds a section at the end that allows you to recap with certainty to ask yourself some important questions, before moving forward in this call to the Office of the Apostle.

I truly honor and appreciate the fact that she shares some of her Supernatural encounters. Many over the years have gotten away from sharing their Supernatural experiences when our LORD GOD JEHOVAH is SUPERNATURAL! We are coming upon an era in time when we shall see many Supernatural demonstrations and we must know what is pure and what are signs and wonders.

2 Thessalonians 2:3-9 (King James Version) 3Let no man deceive you by any means: for that day shall not come, except there come a falling away first, and that man of sin berevealed, the son of perdition; 4Who opposeth and exalteth himself above all that is called God, or that is worshipped; so that he as God sitteth in the temple of God, shewing himself that he is God .5Remember ye not, that, when I was yet with you, I told you these things? 6And now ye know what withholdeth that he might be revealed in his time. 7For the mystery of iniquity doth already work: only he who now letteth will let, until he be taken out of the way. 8And then shall that Wicked be revealed, whom the Lord shall consume with the spirit of his mouth, and shall destroy with the brightness of his coming: 9Even him, whose coming is after the working of Satan with all power and signs and lying wonders.

Apostle Dr. Valerie Jackson takes us on her life's journey through the multiple transformations from trauma to triumph of becoming an Apostle. We see how being truly called, chosen and affirmed by GOD and the leading of Holy Spirit has prepared and trained her over the years from a Private to a General in the Kingdom of GOD. She allows us with great humility, intimacy and transparency to see the good, the bad, the ugly and the indifferent in her life as GOD's Apostle! It does not matter where you are in your journey with GOD in ministry, there is always room for Spiritual growth.

We see the scribe in Apostle Dr. Jackson and the anointing to break yokes that rest upon this book, The True Life of An Apostle, to help the reader realign or shift to where they are supposed to be at this appointed time in the true Kingdom of GOD in the Earth!

Prophet Angela Bland-Chisley, Pastoral Team
Made In His Image International Ministries

CONTENTS

CHAPTERS & BIOGRAPHY

FOREWORD

This book is impactful and eye-opening. You can follow Apostle Jackson's life journey and see how God caused all things to work for her good (Roman 8:28). Her experiences can bring you hope, understanding, and encouragement for your own life as God continues to have you walk the walk of personal development and spiritual maturity. You will learn the pains, disappointments, and setbacks of your life were allowed by God; so, He can ultimately conform you to His character and mindset (Romans 8:29). Like Apostle Jackson states: "God uses life as a sculpting tool to sculpt Christ in you." She clearly lets you know the making and life of an apostle is not about fame and glamour, but about being personally minimized so Christ can be magnified in and through you.

Dr. Rickardo Bodden
Associate Pastor & Chief Operating Officer
Hope Christian Church

INTRODUCTION

As I scribed every word of The True Life of an Apostle, I could not help but reflect on what I survived through the process, and development through many trials and tribulations. Growing up being very shy, rejected, often misunderstood for many years the pains and griefs matured me for this God-given assignment that would become a blessing to many near and far.

In the True Life of an Apostle, I avail my highs and lows on this very complex journey with God. Every word penned is detailed and intimate seasons of my life leading up to and after God called me as His Apostle. The True Life of an Apostle is Truth at its core. I know as you read the events of my story; you will see and come to understand the mind of God when He calls someone, how He allows life and everything you thought was wasted to prepare and equip you for your assignment for His purpose! God uses fragments and broken pieces, and He perfects you as you overcome every obstacle that wanted to kill and destroy your purpose. In the end, you will see that God uses everything for His good to work out.

Chapter One

The Authentication & Seal

First, let us define what an Apostle is and what they are not. The word Apostles derives from the verb "apostello" meant "send away" or "send off," and it conveyed the idea of a personal representative who has the power and authority of the one who sent him. The Hebrew verb describes its emphasis on "commissioning" and "empowering."

In layman's term, an Apostle is a Representative of Jesus Christ. An Apostle is one commissioned and sent to empower and enforce the will of God in the Earth as his or her messenger. Apostles are one of The Foundational Accession Gifts of Christ. The thumb represents the Apostle and is the foundation to the working of the entire hand. It works alongside, touching all, and enabling the other fingers to grip and function.

The index finger represents the Prophet. This finger points the way, being a corrector and a director. They are the ones who unveil the rhema will of God. The middle finger represents the Evangelist. It is the longest finger and reaches out to the world. The Evangelist works together with the Prophet and Pastor. The ring finger represents the Pastor. They are married to the Church and washes the Bride with the Word, so that she will become without spot or wrinkle.

The pinky finger, the smallest of all, represents the Teacher, the one who expounds God's Word. This is the finger which can most easily get into the "ear" of the people. The teacher works in close proximity with and submits to the Pastor.

Apostles govern and pave the way as pioneers. Apostles are not bound by gender, race or status. Apostles are born to be Apostles, chosen by God to execute and operate with The Exousia Authority that has been given to them (Exousia) Delegated Authority. Exousia can also be thought of in terms of jurisdiction or dominion over a certain realm, right, privilege, or ability.

SCRIPTURE EXAMPLES:
Matthew 7:28-29 (Amplified Version)
28 "When Jesus had finished [speaking] these words [on the mountain], the crowds were astonished and overwhelmed at His teaching; 29for He was teaching them as one who had authority [to teach entirely of His own volition], and not as their scribes [who relied on others to confirm their authority]."

Matthew 9:6 (Amplified Version)
6 "But so that you may know that the Son of Man has authority and the power on Earth to forgive sins"—then He said to the paralytic, "Get up, pick up your stretcher and go home."

Jesus commissions and gives this Authority to His Beloved Disciples in *Mark 6:7-9.* And He called the 12 to Himself, and began to send them out two by two, and gave them power over unclean spirits. *8He commanded them to take nothing for the journey except a staff— no bag, no bread, no copper in their money belts— 9 but to wear sandals, and not to put on two tunics.*

Apostles are God's Special Messengers; we see in Apostle Paul's writings he explains briefly who he is.

2 Corinthians 1:1 (Amplified Version Classic)
PAUL, AN apostle (a special messenger) of Christ Jesus by the will of God, and Timothy [our] brother, to the church (assembly) of God, which is at Corinth, and to all the saints (the people of God)

throughout Achaia (most of Greece) …

See, it says an Apostle of Christ not man or woman but of Christ Jesus by the will of God, The Father. No one I mean no should be calling themselves to this Scares Office because someone told you, you were an Apostle, try to buy a Title of an Apostle or sell yourself to the highest bidder to become one. Today's Apostles are the Ascension gift of Jesus Christ Ministry on the Earth. See the example of How and when he gave gifts (Apostles) unto to man.

Ephesians 4:7 (King James Version)
7But grace was given to each one of us according to the measure of Christ's gift.

Therefore, it says, "When he ascended on high, he led a host of captives, and he gave gifts to men."

?

(In saying, "He ascended," what does it mean but that He had also descended into the lower regions, the Earth? He who descended is the one who also ascended far above all the heavens, that He might fill all things).

And He gave the apostles, the prophets, the evangelists, the shepherds and teachers to equip the saints for the work of ministry, for building up the body of Christ, until we all attain to the unity of the faith and of the knowledge of the Son of God, to mature manhood, to the measure of the stature of the fullness of Christ, so that we may no longer be children, tossed to and fro by the waves and carried about by every wind of doctrine, by human cunning, by craftiness in deceitful schemes.

We need Apostles today to continue with The Ministry of Jesus Christ in the Earth, just as we do all the other Ascension Gifts to equip the Saints for the work of ministry. So, for those that believe there are no more Apostles, how will you learn? How will the Body come to the fullness of Christ?

This is where you may want to pause? Am I an Apostle? Do these descriptions relate to me in any way? A couple of main points to look at below:

- Apostles govern:
- Apostles establish:
- Apostles are teachers:
- Apostles equip:
- Apostles delegate,
- Apostles pioneer:
- Apostles plow:
- Apostles commission:
- Apostle suffer greatly:
- Apostles empower:
- Apostles are builders and architects:
- Apostles are visionaries:
- Apostles are resilient:
- Apostles have strong faith:
- Apostles walk in miracles, signs and wonders.
- These are just some of their characteristics.

What an Apostle is not

An Apostle is not a denomination or religious title attached to a particular group or alliance. Apostles are not Appointed by Man but created and Ordained by God. Apostles are people of Structure and Order; they follow the Divine Order established by Jesus Christ concerning the Church of Jesus Christ. They Preach the Apostle's Doctrine not their own. True Apostles do not compromise for platform, fame or fortune. Apostles are not concerned with man's acknowledgements and accolades; their aim is to please God even when they understand it may cause separation and rejection from loved ones. Today many say their Apostles but they're not their more concerned with being served then being a servant, their motivation is driven by people idolizing them, money prestige etc. They want people to see them as being Supreme, not seeing God as the Supreme God.

2 Corinthians 11:13-15 (King James Version)
13For such people are false apostles, deceitful workers, masquerading as apostles of Christ. 14And no wonder, for Satan himself masquerades as an angel of light. 15It is not surprising,

then, if his servants also masquerade as servants of righteousness. Their end will be what their actions deserve.

Please be careful not to fall for the schemes of this day everyone wants to be an Apostle and we must use our divine discernment to discern the truth from a lie. Prayer is very important specifically prayer in the Holy Spirit to receive guidance and revelation.

True Apostles are dedicated to the service of serving Christ first then others.

Romans 12:1-2 (Amplified Version Classic)
Dedicated Service
12 Therefore I urge you, [b]brothers and sisters, by the mercies of God, to present your bodies [dedicating all of yourselves, set apart] as a living sacrifice, holy and well-pleasing to God, which is your rational (logical, intelligent) act of worship. 2And do not be conformed to this world [any longer with its superficial values and customs], but be and progressively changed [as you mature spiritually] by the renewing of your mind [focusing on godly values and ethical attitudes], so that you may prove [for yourselves] what the will of God is, that which is good and acceptable and perfect [in His plan and purpose for you].

As an Apostle of God, called by His grace and equipped by the Power of The Holy Spirit and trained through a life of sufferings. Most people do not have a clue what it means to be chosen by God to be His Apostle. The Office of The Apostle is often looked upon as a hierarchy position or title but, it is considered the least, Jesus confronts His Disciples as they argued about who is the greatest in the Kingdom of God and Jesus replied, "the least is the greatest in the Kingdom". Example: Jesus came to Earth as The Son of God and He was humiliated by the religious leaders, rejected by those He loved, lied on, persecuted and crucified. Basically, He suffered, does this sound like they rolled out the red carpet for Him?

The Making, Molding and Shaping
Genesis 1:27 (King James Version)
27 So God created man in his own image, in the image of God created he

him; male and female created he them.

Let us define the word Making: the act or process of forming, causing, doing, or coming into being.: a process or means of advancement or success.

We were made in The Image and likeness of God, but we have allowed Satan to trick us in believing we are not. So, we constantly live in an old image that represents the own man.

Molding: the act of creating something that is different from the materials that went into it. - the act of creating something by casting it in a mold.

Shaping: develop in a particular way; progress. make (something) fit the form of something else.to decide or influence the form of something, especially a belief or idea, or someone's character.

This part of the process can be painful to the flesh but necessary for our making, The Bible uses Clay as a metaphor of us being pliable to be molded and shaped by life's ups and downs circumstances that God allows us to endure and to overcome.

We are the clay in the potter's hand, and we must go through a process of making molding and shaping the master Potter!

Jeremiah 18:1-6 (King James Version)
18 The word which came to Jeremiah from the Lord, saying, 2Arise, and go down to the potter's house, and there I will cause thee to hear my words. 3Then I went down to the potter's house, and, behold, he wrought a work on the wheels. 4And the vessel that he made of clay was marred in the hand of the potter: so he made it again another vessel, as seemed good to the potter to make it. 5Then the word of the Lord came to me, saying, 6O house of Israel, cannot I do with you as this potter? saith the Lord. Behold, as the clay is in the potter's hand, so are ye in mine hand, O house of Israel.

Let us have some real talk about my life as an Apostle. Growing up in a family of six children, me being the youngest of the six, I learned a lot from life's challenges very early. I heard conversations and saw too much that caused my imagination to be full of images that would limit my productivity in life. Coming from a good home filled with love and a mother and father to nurture me is the greatest memory that one could have. My mom was the greatest and my dad was always supportive of my desires. Early on I dealt with low self-esteem and insecurity issues because of some educational challenges. I missed a lot of school due to illness during my years of puberty. I had the worst menstrual cramps one could ever imagine. I stayed in pain every month when my cycles came. It was so bad that I had to be in the bed most of the time. Oftentimes, I would bleed for weeks, I could not get up or go to school, so I missed a lot of time out of school. When I did go to school, I had bad experiences. I was bullied, mocked and called names. I developed an insecurity about myself that led to low self-esteem and shyness brought on by insecurities in my adult years. I dealt with shyness, rejection and jealousy very badly. These insecurities were caused by childhood and adulthood trauma from physical and mental abuse.

As you can see, the life of an Apostle is not a pretty one. I learned how to be an overcomer through adversity earlier on. My mother laid the foundation, teaching me early on, how to know God and to receive His salvation through believing in His Son, Jesus Christ. She often taught us about believing in the word of God and sending us off to church on Sundays. I grew up in a neighborhood where there was a community church more like the Methodist Denomination. This was the beginning of my Christian education.

The Shaking & The Beating
Despite the foundation that was laid, like any other teenager you want to explore life. As stated earlier, school was not nice to me, so by the time I made it to high school, I was spiraling out of control. I hooked up with friends that had a strong influence on me and shortly after, I started hooking school and missing classes on a regular basis. I was expelled from school due to age and failing grades. I reenrolled myself in The District of Columbia School system, to finish out my high school year was my intention. The Devil had a plan to kill, steal and destroy my destiny; but God also had a plan. It was to prosper me and give me a life of abundance in Him. I got involved with a drug dealer and quickly I was influenced again by a negative voice. I found myself infatuated

with this man. He wined and dined me with all the finer things in life. I thought this was "the good life", we fed each other's weaknesses. He was very insecure, jealous and dominant. The abuse began with yelling, screaming and belittling. It was not long until it turned into physical abuse. I found myself making excuses for him with family, friends and myself. This toxic relationship went on for over 10 years. I later learned that I was pregnant with a child, I felt like I was trapped and had no way of escape. My son was born, and the abuse continued. I started going into depression being in this unhealthy environment. Almost two years have passed, and I find myself with a child yet again, in denial and needing a reality check. I lived a lie telling myself, "I am good", the Devil had me so bound I did not know how to get free. He started treating me nice, and suddenly, I fell for it. I was so blind; the Devil can really confuse you when you do not know who you are. I prayed and prayed I needed a way of escape.

1 Corinthians. 10:13 (New King James Version)
13"No temptation has overtaken you except such as is common to man; but God is faithful, who will not allow you to be tempted beyond what you are able, but with the temptation will also make the way of escape, that you may be able to bear it."

Listen when God gives you a way of escape you better take it, death wanted me, The Devil #1 assignment is to kill us, steal our Soul and to destroy our lives! God's plans are to prosper us and give us a future in Him, but the devils want to blind us of the truth (2 Corinthians 4:4)! The god of this age has blinded the minds of unbelievers, so that they cannot see the light of the gospel that displays the glory of Christ, who is the image of God.

God gave me a way of escape. He got locked up. I finally felt free. I thought to myself, "my life will get back on track." Little did I know what I was dealing with was more than an infatuation, it was a soul tie and a stronghold.

Let me define what a soul tie is:
Soul ties are emotional bonds that form an attachment. They may be godly or ungodly, pure or demonic.

A soul tie is like a linkage in the soul realm between two people. It links their souls together, which can bring forth both beneficial and negative results.

The negative effect of a soul tie: Soul ties can also be used for the devil's advantage. Soul ties formed from sex outside of marriage causes a person to become defiled: Because we had sex outside of marriage, we created an ungodly Soul tie that caused a covenant to be made in our Souls.

I tried to walk away but it was not that simple because the soul tie we created had to be severed and destroyed by renouncing it and repenting to God. Then we had to cast out the Spirits that came along with the sexual soul ties, like lust and perversion. The strongholds had to be destroyed, as well. My mindset needed healing from a faulty way of thinking before I could understand who I was, who God created me to be, and before I could move forward properly.

The Devil never stopped, he wanted to destroy me. It was one battle after another. I experienced more trauma when I was in a car accident in 1991 that left me hospitalized for over 4 months. I had internal bleeding, a collapsed lung, a punctured spleen, a broken wrist, hands, fractured femur and a dislocated hip. While in the hospital, I had a nurse that I will never forget, she was my messenger from God. While on my sick bed she reaches down beside me and tells me, "You're not going to die, God is calling you, you will preach the gospel and operate in the Spirit of God." I am like, "Lady what are you talking about?" I was wowed by her words and never thought anymore about it. My experience was something no one would wish to experience the suffering, my Lord! I had to learn how to walk again. This pain I went through was indescribable. I wanted to die! I had already faced death before.

Somewhere, along the way, I must have experienced brain damage, because I went right back to this unhealthy relationship for about another eight years. Finally, I just had enough of the lies, cheating, house being broken into, death threats, etc... and the life as a drug dealer's girlfriend.

Yet again, I found myself pregnant with a child, vacillating over what should I do, "Oh God, HELP! I am trying to escape" was my prayer. I went to the abortion clinic torn knowing I could not do it. I did not have it in me, but I thought I would never get out of this relationship now, 2 kids and barely surviving. The doctor came in and I burst out crying and said, "No, I can't do it!" I could not do it. I knew it was not right and I loved my unborn child. I never looked back and experienced the worst pregnancy ever. But God showed up at the right time because I almost suffered a nervous breakdown. I said, "I just want to die, I can't take it anymore!" Well, I should not have spoken that. I am like, "I know that there has to be more for me."

Afterwards, I began to date again and fell hard again for yet another "misguided" man. However, this time, he was a master manipulator. The relationship lasted some years, but I decided to break it off. I believe, maybe I am "coming to my senses" at this point, you think! The Devil had my mind.

Galatians 5:1 (King James Version)
Stand fast therefore in the liberty wherewith Christ hath made us free and be not entangled again with the yoke of bondage.

See, when you do not get healed from what wounded you, you repeat the same pattern over and over again it's imperative that you receive your healing and deliverance or else your mind won't allow you to untangle from that yoke.

So, at this point, I am seeking God for guidance when I heard Him say, "You don't know your self-worth!" When you know your self-worth, you will not accept or allow certain cycles and patterns to overtake your life and keep accepting this lifestyle for yourself. I began to go back to church and seek God earnestly, and in doing so, I could hear the voice of God more clearly. I began to ask God for a husband. I told Him, "If you send me a husband, I won't date anymore, but I will wait until I know he's the one."

Chapter Two

The Promise
The Pain

Psalms 37:4-5 (King James Version)
4 Delight thyself also in the Lord: and he shall give thee the desires of thine heart. 5 Commit thy way unto the Lord; trust also in him; and he shall bring it to pass.

I met a man, I was not even looking for one at the time, my focus was on my children, but I had made a promise to God and He kept His promise. So, I met someone, there was no sexual attraction that drew us together. I was minding my own business, when out of the blue he drove up, my sister and I started talking to him and he seemed very nice. He asked for my phone number, so I gave it to him. He called me, nothing but hi and bye, short conversation. I am like, "This is it; I am not sure?" We went out to eat and he tells me he feels a connection, never once did he cross the line, just communication. I was like, "God he is so polite and his mannerisms are like nothing I had ever seen", but he has baggage. He was separated with two kids and I had two kids too, and plenty of baggage myself! I did not want to repeat the same patterns, so I had promised myself and God I would wait on Him. As stated earlier, he was separated from his wife, so I am keeping my distance for a while. However, realizing his divorce is final and waiting to see, if he will become more interested; not just with me, but also my children and my family. Ultimately, asking inwardly, "Is this My husband?"

Well, after two years of dating he asked me to marry him, I accepted, and we began to live our life believing it is going to be blissful. After all, I am on the right path now. I am pregnant with our first child and we find out we are having a boy. We were so happy! The baby was born, and we found out at the second week checkup that something is wrong. We did not know what at the time, but it was serious. Our baby boy had to have a special test. The results came back, and it was his heart. He had to have open heart surgery, can you imagine a baby, open heart surgery! I am devastated, with this process right here. I am learning how to pray against sickness and death in this personal experience. We agree to the surgery. We are so heavy laden with a new marriage, a new baby that is sick, we are overwhelmed with grief. This took a toll on our marriage. We were newlyweds and began to argue about everything. And on top of everything else, we were experiencing financial problems. So, at that moment, we were so overwhelmed, I was almost to the point of a nervous breakdown. We really had to turn to the church for prayer and guidance. God comforted us!

Now, it is 2001 and I am broken before God, I remembered crying out to Him in fervent prayer. I went to church one Sunday and I was so low to the point that I was ready to give up! The Devil had been tormenting me by playing flashbacks of the former life and whispering, "You'll never be happy no matter what you do for God!" I cannot shut off his voice, he kept tormenting me. The Pastor called for an Altar call and I ran to the altar crying profusely, the Pastor says, "Anyone who wants to be filled with The Baptism of the Holy Spirit today -- you can be."

Matthew 5:6 (King James Version)
Blessed are they which do hunger and thirst after righteousness: for they shall be filled.
Don't you want to be filled with God's Spirit then you must be thirsty for it, I was thirsty and empty. I needed an infilling of the manifestation of His Spirit to strengthen me inwardly. The Comforter will come and live inside of us when we allow our spirit to open-up. I was so broken it was a life or death encounter I had to have right in that moment. I repented of all my sin and cried out to the Lord and He heard my cry and rescued me.

There were so many people at the altar I never forgot, they were leaving unfilled, my mind was made up, I am not leaving, I am going to be filled today! I kept crying out to God, church was coming to an end, but I stayed at the altar. An Evangelist came and prayed with me, I will never forget her words, she said, "You must surrender everything to God today!" I said, "God I will, and I trust you," instantly, He fills me with the Baptism of The Holy Spirit! I felt nothing but FIRE that clove my whole entire body, especially my tongue. I fell to the floor after being filled, my Pastor later told me, I had an overflow encounter, he said he never saw anything like it.

Afterwards, I knew my life would never be the same, it changed my life completely!

THE REVEALING
From that day forth, I could feel the Hand of God in my life. Words can't explain how I was feeling.

My Spiritual Gifts began to surface. I could hear the voice of God so much clearly. I had dreams and visions almost every day after my Holy Ghost endowment! I would meet people that I never knew and could tell them what they were dealing with, how they were feeling and so forth. I could see the heart, pain and hidden agendas. I was a novice; I did not know what was happening to me.

The dreams were so intense, I would dream about people, places and events all over the world! I would see myself in dreams praying for people and they were being healed.

Now, before anyone taught me anything about praying, The Holy Spirit taught me how to pray, I would pray in The Holy Spirit all the time, I was getting stronger and wiser as I prayed. I would feel a strong unction to pray for people especially those that had mental or physical issues. Prayer quickly became my passion. There was something about prayer, I felt it was my calling to pray. I found myself having a feeling that would come over me for people who were sick or hurting. I wanted to help them.

God was developing my sensitivity in the Spirit, everything was happening so fast, I felt I had no one to talk to! I really did not trust my Pastor. I forgot to mention as my gifts were being perfected in the process, I began to see the leader's shortcomings, as a novice, I did not know what to do, so I talked to God. However, this made me very uncomfortable. I kept it to myself.

Someone reading this today, maybe experiencing similar experiences, and you feel confused and embarrassed to talk to someone about it, first thing you should do is seek The Lord in prayer next ask The Lord to give you clarity and revelation of what you're seeing never jump to any conclusions that what you're seeing is interpreted with the eyes of God, make sure that there's nothing in your heart towards that individual, leader that you're seeing this way you will not be prejudice or bias when God really begins to show even more sensitive things.

Divine Connection
Jeremiah 29:11-13 (English Standard Version)
For I know the plans I have for you, declares the Lord, plans for welfare and not for evil, to give you a future and a hope. Then you will call upon me and come and pray to me, and I will hear you. You will seek me and find me when you seek me with all your heart.

God's Timing is always on Time! Sometimes, we get anxious and in a hurry and want God to move like yesterday but our God knows the exact timing for every event to occur in our lives the days the times the places the people ...this is God being all wise and all knowing. He knows our future, as well as, our beginning. He knows every plan, every strategy and everything that's needed to for us to fulfill His Will.

And as it relates to the journey, He created us so, He knows how long it is going to take us to get there. As well as, what detours we will make on the way and any interferences or roadblocks that we may encounter; but it does not negate the fact that God will perfect those things that concern us -- in His Time not ours.

The church I was attending at this time was a traditional church, you know the ones who did not believe in women wearing pants, women should wear hats on their heads when they pray, and women should keep silent extra. But there were some positives to the church. It was a Holy Spirit filled church with constant prayer meetings. Here is where God sets me up. I met this young lady at the church that I am attending, she seemed nice and friendly, but then I noticed I did not see her anymore after a while. I found out that she had left the church because there was a misunderstanding that caused friction. Anyway, she comes back one Sunday just for me as she stated, she said to me, "Has anyone ever told you there's a call on your life and you'll preach?" I am just staring at her like, I cannot believe it, I had forgotten all about what the nurse told me in 1991 after my car accident. So, she invites me to her church. I go and it's a Wednesday night Bible Study, I am so nervous. Worship is so High; I had never experienced that kind of worship before. I am feeling so blessed to be there and out of nowhere the Pastor calls me out to the altar, I went, and he tells me, "You're not crazy, you do hear from God clearly and you see dreams and vision regularly!" I was shocked like, God how does he know all of this? I am crying so full of joy like, "At last, somebody understands me and what's going on in me!"

I quickly went home and told my husband; we came back next Sunday and the following Sunday. We decided to join the church. I am finally feeling blessed in a new church, learning new things about The Holy Spirit and the gifts of the Spirit.

We took this gift test, I will never forget it, and it comes back. I fit almost all the categories especially of the Prophet, and Apostle I did not even know what a prophet or an Apostle really was at that time.

I am now in a prophetic church where almost the whole church could prophesy in words or song. It is a Company of Prophets, and my Pastor begins to train me by having me pray and sometimes prophesy without warning. He was a Great Apostolic Teacher and a Prophet. I quickly became interested in who I was as the gifts were intensifying even the more.
God was wowing me big time; I am finally somewhere that I feel like I really belong and not feeling like an oddball. Everyone had some degree of knowledge of The Prophetic.

The Dreamer/The Weeping Prophet

I began to read and research the scriptures. One day I was sleeping, and I had this very intense dream about a lady in my neighborhood that was on crack cocaine. I would often see her walking up and down the street. I always prayed and talked with God about her. So, I dreamt this intense dream about her dying and the Spirit of God spoke to me saying, "She will die If she doesn't repent and come out of those streets!" I woke up terrified, I called this neighborhood evangelist that would house them sometimes for her. I did not want to tell someone that they would die if they did not obey God's voice. I did what God told me to do and the power of God fell upon the church so heavy and on her. She obeyed for a while but went right back out there. I had not talked to or heard about her for almost a year, when I saw the Evangelist and she said, "The lady you gave the prophecy to die because she didn't heed to the word you released to her!" Oh, my goodness I am devastated I could not believe it!

I never wanted to prophesy again! My Pastor said, "You are God's mouthpiece, you must continue to speak for God, or you'll be judged for disobedience!" I did not want to be disobedient to God, so I prayed and got back into alignment with His will. Now I could understand how Prophet Jeremiah felt. Jeremiah was called by God to pronounce judgement to stiff neck people. He became weary in doing well like me and did not want to prophesy anymore because of the type of prophecy that God had called him to deliver.

Jeremiah 20:9 (King James Version)
Then I said, "I will not make mention of Him, nor speak any more in His name." But His word was in mine heart as a burning fire shut up in my bones; and I was weary with forbearing, and I could not hold back.

It became evident at that time, who I was. People were looking for prophecy and prayer on a regular basis. My gift and calling were being stretched. I developed a greater passion for prayer.

God began to give me strategies and guidance on how to pray effectively. Through prayer, He began to give me visions on what He wanted me to do. He gave me a desire to help those that could not help themselves. I found myself in the streets ministering to people, praying, prophesying to them and seeing instant deliverance. Now, I am not at all educated yet on deliverance.

Prophets sometimes have hard messages to release to people that can make you feel uncomfortable at times, but we must obey God's commands. Maybe, God has given you a message of warning for someone and you allowed fear to overtake you. God still sends warnings we see here where God sent Prophet Isaiah to King Hezekiah in 2 Kings 20:1-2. Just like he did with me to the lady that refused to obey.

2 Kings 20:1-2 (King James Version)
In those days Hezekiah became ill and was near death. The prophet Isaiah son of Amoz came to him, and said to him, "Thus says the Lord: Set your house in order, for you shall die and not live." 2Then he turned his face toward the wall and prayed to the Lord, saying, 3"Please, O Lord, remember how I have walked before You faithfully and with an undivided heart and have done what is good in Your sight." And Hezekiah wept bitterly.

"Get your House In Order!"
This was the message from God through the Prophet Isaiah to King Hezekiah who was sick unto death. Oh, what a message to deliver.

Hezekiah received a warning that said "get your house in order" because death is knocking at your door. These messages are never popular, but God chooses those whom he tries to deliver them.

We must heed to the word of The Prophets God sends to warn us. Today many refuse the warnings God sends through his Prophets and sadly face the repercussions of disobedience. God is merciful to them that repent and turn away from Sin. Do not be like many in the Bible that didn't obey God through the Prophet's word.

Matthew 10:41-42 (New King James Version)
41He who receives a prophet in the name of a prophet shall receive a prophet's reward. And he who receives a righteous man in the name of a righteous man shall receive a righteous man's reward. 42And whoever gives one of these little ones only a cup of cold water in the

name of a disciple, assuredly, I say to you, he shall by no means lose his reward.

Ready or Not here, I come!
My first time experiencing a demon was when I was about 14 years old my father and I was held up in my basement by my brother's friend that was high off some drugs he had taken. Somehow, he got into our house and locked my father and I in the basement his eyes changed dark, and he begins to growl I had never seen anything like it before! I don't fully remember all the details, but my brother came home and called the police. They came and rescued us. Thank God. I heard stories about demons and witchcraft from my mom. Her mother was poisoned by her own cousin who worked witchcraft on her, and she became so sickly and later died. My mom would tell us to be very careful of eating everyone's food and be cautious of receiving gifts and tokens from people with the wrong spirit. Some of what was shared with me early helped groomed me for awareness today.

The very first time I met deliverance head on was so unexpected my Pastor called me and one of the brothers up to pray for this lady one Sunday in Worship Service, this lady was slivering on the floor like a snake, making all kinds of hissing sounds. Believe it or not, for some reason, I wasn't frightened or scared at all. I quickly began praying in the Holy Ghost and laid hands on her head, along with the brother that was assisting me in the deliverance. She started vomiting up mucus and shaking uncontrollably and could not breathe until she collapsed. I thought, oh my goodness, we have killed her. Remember, I am a novice, no one has ever trained me. I was thrown into it without any warning. When she came to, she looked beautiful, her complexion was lighter, and she was full of joy. No more hissing she was fully aware of her surroundings. I was amazed, really amazed!

Today, I now know that Spirit was a Python Spirit and Spirit of Leviathan, which is very dominant. No one can or should attempt to work deliverance at any degree without, number one the guidance of the Holy Spirit, proper training and a Team of Intercessor or Prayer Warriors that are ministry-trained and highly fluent in the Gift of Discerning of Spirits.

Ephesians 6:12 (King James Version)
For we wrestle not against flesh and blood, but against principalities, against powers, against the rulers of the darkness of this world, against spiritual wickedness in high places.

Please do not be ignorant to the fact that demonic influence exists in today's world many people have been wounded, deceived and tricked and some killed by the ignorance of believing that these manifestations of darkness do not exist. That is why it's imperative to read your Bible. As an Apostle of God, I love to teach, train and equip believers to become Deliverance Ministers.

My first time was an unexpected deliverance, following that episode there was nowhere I could go without demons manifesting and crying out. My gift of discerning of spirits along with my prophetic senses, I could smell the stench of demons in the atmosphere. Oftentimes, I would get nauseous from the smell.

Not only was I able to smell demonic spirits, but I could also sense them. I knew when they were near. I would get nauseous, especially someone with a terminal illness, I could smell death. It was so weird to me, no one ever taught me about my gifts at this time. I was clueless until I started researching and ready. It did not matter how much I had learned from books the Holy Spirit was my ultimate helper in times of deliverance.

I could never understand someone claiming to be an Apostle or a believer and don't believe in deliverance and casting out demons. I have heard some say, "It's a mind over matter situation". Some even frown their noses up at the thought of deliverance. There are things that only Holy Spirit can teach, especially concerning supernatural things. Jesus had so much opposition particularly when he would cast out demons.

Apostles have power and Authority to cast out demonic spirits, demons and over demonic atmospheres and regions that have been assigned to us. The Greek define this power Exousia: is power, authority, control, dominion, sway delegated authority. The other word is dunamis: miraculous) power, might, strength.

Usage: (a) physical power, force, might, ability, efficacy, energy, meaning (b) plur: powerful deeds, deeds showing (physical) power, marvelous works.

Mark 16:17 (New Living Translation)
These miraculous signs will accompany those who believe: They will cast out demons in my name, and they will speak in new languages.

Deliverance is a benefit from Jesus Christ. It is nothing to be embarrassed about; it's the Love of God for His children for us to be free. In fact, that's why Jesus came to set the captives free from bondage. I never felt judgmental towards anyone. I was completely compassionate about seeing them set free by The Power of God, the one that works because deliverance must be merciful, compassionate and display The Love of God.

Chapter Three

The Process Begins

There were so many things beginning to take place in my life that I was still at the point where I was trying to process everything. And things were moving so fast. God was accelerating the pace and I was beginning to grow and become wiser and more knowledgeable in specific areas.

As time progressed and God was cultivating me, my leaders became agitated at times with me. I could see it and sense it. It was heartbreaking because I loved my leaders and was very faithful in serving and honoring them. I felt God nudging me. I did not know what it meant. I could not explain it or articulate completely in words, but it was consistent. It never stopped. I knew I had to find out what it was that God was trying to convey to me. I did not know what to do. there was one time my leader asked if God was calling me. At that time, I really didn't know for sure even though I was feeling a pull outside of the church I was attending. I began to go to church and felt on the outside until one day It got harder and harder for me to be in attendance there. It was strange I could not fully understand it. I tried as hard as I could to keep pressing to be there, but God was calling me out and I had to obey Him. Every message that I began to hear felt like a personal attack on me for my obedience to God. It was as if I was a target; so, I constantly cried out and prayed to God because it was becoming so unbearable for me to be there. So, I said God if it be your will please give me a sign and surely I will obey. And one day, I decided to go to a Friday night service at another church and when altar call came I went up for prayer and the Pastor said to me Woman of God it is a decision that you have been contemplating on and the Lord said it is time for you to make a move on that decision and it's okay with him, you can go!

Oh my Goodness, I was at so relieved; it was if God had told him the story and gave him the answers that I was looking for. This was my release that I could go without guilt, knowing that it was truly my time. I told my leader I was leaving, and it did not go over as well as I had hoped, but I had to obey God's voice. It was hard when people talked about us leaving and saying I was rebellious and moving out of God's timing, but I heard God's voice clearly.

As I obeyed God to do His will, OMG! All hell started to break loose in my world. Family members became angry towards me, lied on me and my husband to friends and neighbors, trying to destroy our character and our name with slander, but we overcame the Devil's games. As you can see, there is a lot you must process, it is bad enough that you have to deal with unrighteous people in the world; but even worse when you are being attacked by self-righteous believers. One of the things even before answering the call of any calling that God is calling you to you must endure a very strategic process that God allows that is a hard pill to swallow God allows it just like he allowed Daniel to go into the lion's den just like he allows Jonah to be swallowed in the belly of the whale just like he allowed Joseph to be put in the pit, just like he allowed David to get in the King's Palace. Keep in mind, all of the process is in the will of God -- never fight your process!

Divine processes are necessary! God will always be with you through your process. Remember, the word of God says he will never leave you or forsake you. This means doing the hardest times of your life and your valley experiences God will be with you even in the valley He is with you in the lowest times. You must go through this process that is so necessary for you becoming who he has called you to be. The process will position you and posture you when you are set in your function as an apostle or any 5-Fold Leader. Divine processes give you endurance and fortification in your function.

The Investment

It was imperative that I began to invest more in my gifts, wanting to be educated and proficient in my understanding of how The Ministry of The Holy Spirit operated in the believer's life. I went to seminars, The School of Prophets, Deliverance Trainings and Intercessory Trainings, you name it! I believe you can be anointed, but lack understanding and the word of the Lord tells us in

Proverbs 4:7 (King James Version)
Wisdom is the principal thing; therefore get wisdom: and with all thy getting, get understanding.

In learning the Ministry of The Holy Spirit, it was always taught to yield to the leading and guiding of The Holy Spirit, this made ministry a whole lot easier once I learned that He works through us when we allow Him.

So, all the studies that I acquired were not the essence of moving in the Apostleship, it was the Life of Sufferings I had to endure that equipped me for Apostolic works to be truly honest. Now this does not mean that you do not sit and be taught by others. It means that your life lessons are a vital part of your journey. I did not wake up one day and decide to be God's Apostle; it was predestined by God himself.

Apostles suffer a great deal of pain throughout life, but must remain resilient, meaning easily bouncing back as a Good Soldier of Christ. It is the life lessons, sufferings and as you are tried and tested bearing the marks of an Apostle, as Paul said in the book of Galatians 6:17. We see Apostle Paul was an Apostle that had many challenges in life, he faced a shipwreck on one of his missions. Even then He was determined to The Will of God. Apostles do not have to prove themselves to anyone, the evidence of The Marks will be upon them as they continue on this Apostolic journey.

Galatians 6:17 (Amplified Classic Edition)
From now on let no one trouble me [by making it necessary for me to justify my authority as an apostle, and the absolute truth of the gospel], for I bear on my body the [a]branding-marks of Jesus [the wounds, scars, and other outward evidence of persecutions—these

testify to His ownership of me].

Lord, have mercy! I know about the wounds and the scars too well! From a child I suffered persecution, bullying, mocking etc. God had to deliver me from so much in life, to name a few struggles and strongholds like rejection, low self-esteem, shyness and insecurities, jealousy and despair. So, let me say this, please before stepping into your place of Leadership, please get your proper healing and deliverance. We cannot help anyone until we surrender our own demons to The Lord! Oftentimes we believe no one can see our pain well there's people that can. There is no shame in being weak or broken therefore Jesus Christ came to bind up the wounds that we have. No one I mean no one is expected to be fully arrived. Remember Paul said it. There is a pressing towards the prize in Christ Jesus, and I am continuously forgetting those things which are behind and pressing forward. Keeping a Focus on The Prize will be challenging at times, but He gives you the strength to do it! So now I am delivered and healthy and God calls me to establish a Church, this is the next chapter.

1 Peter 2:9 (English Standard Version)
But you are a chosen race, a royal priesthood, a holy nation, a people for his own possession, that you may proclaim the excellencies of him who called you out of darkness into his marvelous light.

Everything we go through is to proclaim the excellencies of Him who called us! After the process you will know rather or not you have been truly called! If your still standing firm after all the trials and tribulations that should have killed, you and caused you to lay down and do not get back up these are one of the signs you are called and chosen with great purpose.

Do not fear or be afraid to say yes to God because you must be fortified to be a front-liner.

Deuteronomy 31:8 (English Standard Version)
It is the Lord who goes before you. He will be with you; he will not leave you or forsake you. Do not fear or be dismayed."

THE VISION/AFFIRMATION
Habbakuk 2:1-3 (King James Version)
I will stand upon my watch, and set me upon the tower, and will watch to see what he will say unto me, and what I shall answer when I am reproved. 2And the Lord answered me, and said, Write the vision, and make it plain upon tables, that he may run that readeth it. 3For the vision is yet for an appointed time, but at the end it shall speak, and not lie: though it tarry, wait for it; because it will surely come, it will not tarry.

God gives me another dream this time; it is about where He wants us to go and establish the church. In the dream He tells me to tell my husband to ask the owner of a boxing gym, if we can use it to hold Sunday services. I could not believe God was directing us to go into a gym, this went against everything we were taught, like God did not call anyone to start a storefront church, God tells your Pastor where your church will be etc. After the dream I waited at first to tell my husband, but I have another dream, so I said I better tell him. God dealt with me a lot in dreams.

Most of my calling initially came by way of dream communication. Then by revelations and confirmations one after another. So, I told my husband and here his response. My husband said, "A gym for Sunday services?" I said, "Yes-- that's what the Lord said to me!" He could not believe it like me that God was calling us to have Sunday services in a Gym. He asked him and not only did he say yes, but he also brought us the chairs and tables to conduct services. This was a Jewish millionaire. Look at God! He tells us there is no charge, just use it as long as you want.

We are new Pastors with zeal and fire, God begins to send who He wants. We begin to get families and teenagers and they receive the Lord Jesus Christ as their Lord and Savior!! Yes Lord, they are saved by the Power of God and in two to three years, we baptized over 25 people, mostly teenagers. We found ourselves working deliverance every Sunday. This is super exciting for us to see tangible things taking place rapidly and consistently despite all the naysayers and the negative feedback that we constantly receive from not people in the world but yet people that proclaim to know Jesus and have a relationship with Him see you must understand when you know that God has called you, equip you and qualified you, you must not get caught up in the words of naysayers, naysayers are planted by Satan to convince you to forfeit the promises of God you know that God has not only promise you what He would do but has made it tangible for you to be able to do it. When God has a plan and a mandate for anyone's life, He already has the blueprint.

I feel like taking a pause right here and pray for someone that God has spoken to and you know God has spoken to you he is given you the vision, you wrote it down it is speaking to you right now it is very plain but for some reason your stagnated with running with it Fear must leave, you are battling fear... I say to you this day take the vision, read it again and allow those that can see the vision like you they'll help you run with it. Stop sharing it with blind people that have no sight! God is sending someone that will see the vision as clear as you and help you build and run with it! I want to pray for you now father in the name of Jesus I believe I believe in this person that is reading this book right now I believe in the power of God to transcend upon this person right now and the power of God Ignite them with fire to get tenacity to build in the Mighty name of Jesus Christ. Get ready as you continue read these words off this page that something inside of you will activate and caused you to become alive and believe again in the vision that they put down and they forgot about I prophesied now that you will pick up the vision again and you will run with it and it will accomplish all that God has purposed for it to accomplish in your due season in Jesus mighty name! I believe it and declare it to be so my friend.

People begin to hear about us and before you knew it, we were known as The House of Deliverance. People came from other churches to be healed and delivered by the Power of The Holy Spirit. God had His hand on our Ministry and on us. We were so blessed! We would feed and help people with their bills, etc. We became like a Mother and Father to many. People were still mocking us and making fun of us because we did not have a church building with all the bells and whistles, but it was evident that God's Spirit was present! Tangible signs, miracles and wonders were taking place and God's love was drawing them in every Sunday. This was God all the way, we stayed there almost four years and we did not feel compelled to go; because it seemed to be the dwelling place where God abided. People would come from church all over to see what was happening in this basement/gym. Testimonies were going out left and right. We began to face so much opposition from others that wanted to use the space we had. After a while we left and moved to another location that was not as fruitful. It is very important you be only where God needs you to be.

As a female, I caught a lot of grief everywhere I went to minister. They would never call me Pastor, Prophet and especially, not Apostle. It was a gender barrier to them. So, they would call me Evangelist because they felt that an Evangelist or Missionary was a more feminine office for a woman, than any of the others, crazy right?

We must understand there is no gender in the spirit, God is not looking for a male or a female He is looking for a willing vessel male or female to do His bidding on the Earth. We must stop debating about this and grid up our loins. We have work to do! Our number one focus must always remain doing the work of the Lord without compromising or without malice in our heart but, yet our focus is to aim to please our God with everything that we do it unto the Lord.

So, I go to minister out of state one day and an Apostle says to me, "Has anyone ever told you that you're an Apostle called by God?" I said, "No, I've been called many things but never an Apostle!" So, I began to talk to God about The Office of the Apostle because he has me curious now.

Please seek, and talk (have a conversation) with God through prayer particularly, when you get personal prophecies. Make sure that the person's fruit and spirit is intact and that there are no hidden agendas or motives behind the personal prophecy that's being released. Making certain that you use your God-given discernment to discern if is this is a true word from God, as well as, determining what spirit is attached. This can be done by going into your time of prayer with the Lord and he will reveal truth to you in reference to any prophecies that you make it get on a personal level. Rule of thumb, never just receive the word without having the word judged.

A lot of people crave for this position and function to be an Apostle and I believe we have more imposters than we do Apostles' not saying it to sound condescending, but to be brutally honest; there are so many people claiming to be Apostles today but, yet do not represent the kingdom with the evidence of the fruit. I never dreamed of being an Apostle. I never thought I would be one even as I came into ministry. I never desired it, but it was what God had pre-Destin and his will. I could no longer deny it; it was not one of those things where you are obsessed about. Most people that are called to this Apostleship is not because they desire it. I am fine doing what I am doing for God! I am not driven by a title; I just love God and know He has called me. So, one day I am out again at another Service and I get called out. The Apostle says, "You in the white, come here!" So, I am like, Lord okay, so now He tells me, "You're called to operate in the Supernatural and I see a strong Anointing on you as an Apostle with a Prophets mantle." I say, "Okay!" So, me always wanting to hear straight from God myself, I did not rush or move straight until something special happened.

Oftentimes, people move into an Office just because prophecies come. I was accustomed to God confirming with me by way of dreams and the written word, so I said, "You'll tell me when it's time!" It started to become evident. I noticed a great shift with Leaders looking up to me for Guidance and Counsel on a regular basis. I found myself doing more mentoring and cultivating with leadership more than I imagined. Helping to establish churches and ministries throughout the East Coast and counseling more than over 25 pastors a year. It was evident God was perfecting His Grace upon my Apostolic Authorities concerning men in the Kingdom of God. Much of the work I have done has never gotten recognition for as Paul states, "I am the least of the Apostles", in my circle of Influence, though I have done great works. Apostle Paul stated, "Not I but Christ in me doeth the works." See true Apostles understand it is not about recognition from man but from God and we are known as Bonds Servants.

Ephesians 3:8 (New King James Version)
Though I am less than the least of all the saints, this grace was given me: to preach to the Gentiles the unsearchable riches of Christ.

So, my hunger grew stronger for teachings on the Body of Christ and how there was a great need for developing Saints in their Offices. I began identifying those that walked in The Five-Fold and began to help train them for the up building in the Kingdom of God. Now I am starting to experience some of the prophecies that have been spoken over the years come to pass.

Chapter Four

The Call

1 Corinthians 1:1 (New King James Version)
Paul, called to be an apostle of Jesus Christ through the will of God, and
Sosthenes our brother.

I had a dream over years later, it is very confusing at first, but in the dream these men came to get me from the car shop where my car is being fixed and they call me by name, my whole name. I said, "Who are you and how did you know I was here", they said, "God sent us to get you, come with us." I was terrified in the dream, but I went. We started walking and the street appears to be covered with ancient rocks like pavement in the biblical days. We get to our destination and there are thousands of people all dressed in beautiful robes, women and men waiting on me. There were two older gentlemen, they grabbed my arm and drenched me in water, like an emerging and then I woke up.

I had no clue what it meant. Weeks later an Apostle comes to me in person and says to me, "God did it already, Apostle!" I said, "Did what?" He said, "Ordained you and set you apart, as His Apostle!" I was blown, only God could have shared the dream with him. When he started telling me I couldn't believe it, God showed him!

Five years after that went by, God said, "It was time!" He said, "I have been training you, your whole life for this place, now you have to realize it!" It was years later, after the prophecy that I received on three different occasions. However, it was not until I had the dream and encounter with God that I realized He called me to The Apostleship. Not man, but God! He's using men to Affirm and Confirm in the Earth, but it is He who calls us.

Apostle's Affirmation and confirmation came in a unique way we all know the story about the apostle Paul on the road to Damascus how he had to be blinded and knocked off at his horse to answer the call of the Apostle fay guy was calling him to then sound like a pretty picture to me well most likely all of us that are called to this particular Scares office go through similar situations metaphorically speaking that is. Let us read how Apostle Paul received his calling.

Acts 9:1-31 (New International Version)
Saul's Conversion

> *9 Meanwhile, Saul was still breathing out murderous threats against the Lord's disciples. He went to the high priest 2and asked him for letters to the synagogues in Damascus, so that if he found any there who belonged to the Way, whether men or women, he might take them as prisoners to Jerusalem. 3As he neared Damascus on his journey, suddenly a light from heaven flashed around him. 4He fell to the ground and heard a voice say to him, "Saul, Saul, why do you persecute me?"*
>
> *5"Who are you, Lord?" Saul asked. "I am Jesus, whom you are persecuting," he replied. 6"Now get up and go into the city, and you will be told what you must do." 7The men traveling with Saul stood there speechless; they heard the sound but did not see anyone. 8Saul got up from the ground, but when he opened his eyes he could see nothing. So they led him by the hand into Damascus. 9For three days he was blind, and did not eat or drink anything. 10In Damascus there was a disciple named Ananias. The Lord called to him in a vision, "Ananias!" "Yes, Lord," he answered. 11The Lord told him, "Go to the house of Judas on Straight Street and ask for a man from Tarsus named Saul, for he is praying. 12In a vision he has seen a man named Ananias come and place his hands on him to restore his sight." 13 "Lord," Ananias answered, "I have heard many reports about*

this man and all the harm he has done to your holy people in Jerusalem. 14And he has come here with authority from the chief priests to arrest all who call on your name." 15But the Lord said to Ananias, "Go! This man is my chosen instrument to proclaim my name to the Gentiles and their kings and to the people of Israel. 16I will show him how much he must suffer for my name." 17Then Ananias went to the house and entered it. Placing his hands on Saul, he said, "Brother Saul, the Lord— Jesus, who appeared to you on the road as you were coming here—has sent me so that you may see again and be filled with the Holy Spirit." 18Immediately, something like scales fell from Saul's eyes, and he could see again. He got up and was baptized, 19and after taking some food, he regained his strength.

Saul in Damascus and Jerusalem

Saul spent several days with the disciples in Damascus:
20At once he began to preach in the synagogues that Jesus is the Son of God. 21All those who heard him were astonished and asked, "Isn't he the man who raised havoc in Jerusalem among those who call on this name? And hasn't he come here to take them as prisoners to the chief priests?" 22Yet Saul grew more and more powerful and baffled the Jews living in Damascus by proving that Jesus is the Messiah.23After many days had gone by, there was a conspiracy among the Jews to kill him, 24but Saul learned of their plan. Day and night they kept close watch on the city gates in order to kill him. 25But his followers took him by night and lowered him in a basket through an opening in the wall. 26When he came to Jerusalem, he tried to join the disciples, but they were all afraid of him, not believing that he really was a disciple. 27But Barnabas took him and brought him to the apostles. He told them how Saul on his journey had seen the Lord and that the Lord had spoken to him, and how in Damascus he had preached fearlessly in the name of Jesus. 28So Saul stayed with them and moved about freely in Jerusalem, speaking boldly in the name of the Lord. 29He talked and debated with the Hellenistic Jews, but they tried to kill him. 30When the believers learned of this, they took him down to Caesarea and sent him off to Tarsus. 31Then the church throughout Judea, Galilee and Samaria enjoyed a time of peace and was strengthened. Living in the fear of the Lord and encouraged by the Holy Spirit, it increased in numbers.

God calls all of us in His own way. This was the way He called Saul, whose name was later changed to Paul, after His conversion. You see how Paul was a strong Teacher as well as, a Scribe. Most Apostles are strong Teachers and Scribes. Apostles are Architects they build and establish with great vision. I can remember God telling me, "You're going to start a Deliverance Ministry that travels the world!" I am like, "Really -- Lord, okay!" I had no clue how I would do it, how I would finance it; but when God has a purpose and plan, He always provides the means. I obeyed and launched my first Travel in the state of VA and watched God's miracles unfold.

That same year my mother died suddenly, and I was devastated. The enemy wanted me to cancel the conference, but I knew God would sustain me through this tough time. I kept planning and God prevailed against all the enemy's plans. You see, Apostles are resilient; they are made to endure hardship. I could not dare disappoint God or the people. I had been chosen to do the work. My pain was not enough to stop me, because God's Grace is sufficient. People's lives were blessed and transformed because I knew I was called to endure hardship as a good soldier and that God's strength would be made perfect in my weakness!

2 Timothy 2:1-4 (New King James Version)
You therefore, my son, be strong in the grace that is in Christ Jesus. 2And the things that you have heard from me among many witnesses, commit these to faithful men who will be able to teach others also. 3You therefore must endure[a] hardship as a good soldier of Jesus Christ. 4 No one engaged in warfare entangles himself with the affairs of this life, that he may please him who enlisted him as a soldier.

I often found myself experiencing major warfare every time God gave me major assignments. The devil hated me for my obedience to God. He tried repeatedly to destroy me. It never stopped just because I decided to follow Jesus, now in fact it grew worse. I became a greater threat to him and his Kingdom. These trials taught me how to battle in The Spirit and how to use my Apostolic Authority while engaging in battle.

Ephesians 6:11-18 (New King James Version)
11Put on the whole armor of God, that you may be able to stand against the [a]wiles of the devil. 12For we do not wrestle against flesh and blood, but against principalities, against powers, against the rulers of [b]the darkness of this age, against spiritual hosts of wickedness in the heavenly places. 13Therefore take up the whole armor of God, that you may be able to withstand in the evil day, and having done all, to stand. 14Stand therefore, having girded your waist with truth, having put on the breastplate of righteousness, 15and having shod your feet with the preparation of the gospel of peace; 16above all, taking the shield of faith with which, you will be able to quench all the fiery darts of the wicked one. 17And take the helmet of salvation, and the sword of the Spirit, which is the word of God; 18praying always with all prayer and supplication in the Spirit, being watchful to this end with all perseverance and supplication for all the saints.

As a Deliverance Minister, God would often unction me to go certain places at specific times. Sometimes in the middle of the day, He would say, "Go here, go there", and I would go sensing there was an assignment awaiting me when I got there. Let me give you an example: I went to the Giant Grocery Store as He had instructed, and this lady was walking up and down the aisles screaming and talking out her mind with a large suitcase, instantly I discerned a Spirit of torment, tormenting her. I went where she was and started praying in the spirit and telling torment to "Lose her now, in Jesus' name!" Peace overtook her. Keep in mind that I am in the grocery store! Anyway, that Spirit had to obey and submit to the God in me.

The demons knew who I was, they started trembling because they knew that they would be exposed. I would often get invited to churches to minister anniversary services, pastoral appreciation services, etc., but the result in the end would be a Healing and Deliverance Service. I mean I could not go anywhere and just be Valerie. I would have dinner with my family and The Holy Spirit would say, "Tell the lady sitting to your far left, I am going to heal her", out of nowhere.

Matthew 10:5-10 (New King James Version)
5"These twelve Jesus sent out and commanded them, saying: "Do not go into the way of the Gentiles, and do not enter a city of the Samaritans. 6But go rather to the lost sheep of the house of Israel.
48

7And as you go, preach, saying, 'The kingdom of heaven is at hand.' 8Heal the sick, cleanse the lepers, raise the dead, cast out demons. Freely you have received, freely give. 9Provide neither gold nor silver nor copper in your money belts, 10nor bag for your journey, nor two tunics, nor sandals, nor staffs; for a worker is worthy of his food."

The knowing grew stronger and stronger the more I obeyed His voice, He began to trust me the more with knowledge and His wisdom. All the while I am just honored to serve. People from other ministries would often reach out to me for prayer, guidance and insight for their lives, business ventures etc. I never asked for any offerings or favors I just wanted to serve, it became somewhat overwhelming as more and more people from other ministries were reaching out.

Galatians 6:9 (King James Version)
9And let us not be weary in well doing: for in due season we shall reap, if we faint not.

See like Jesus, He was called to the multitude not just church folks; I quickly learned that He did not call me to have a large church, but He did call me to minister to the multitude.

THE EXPLANATION!

Acts 9:15 (New King James Version)
15But the Lord said to him, "Go, for he is a chosen vessel of Mine to bear My name before Gentiles, kings, and the children of Israel. 16For I will show him how many things he must suffer for My name's sake."

Everything that you will experience on this journey will eventually work in your favor as for the good, the bad, and the ugly. God's purpose and plan is much bigger than the problems. One thing is for sure, the Promises of God remain Yes and Amen!

Jeremiah 29:11 (New King James Version)
11For I know the thoughts that I think toward you, says the Lord, thoughts of peace and not of evil, to give you a future and a hope.

So, every season is different, but they all serve as a major role in molding you as His Apostle. The Lord tells Ananias to tell Apostle Paul, "You will suffer many things." Indeed, you will suffer many things, I am a living witness! You see, it is a false misconception about the lives of Apostles. I am not against prosperity at all, but too much emphasis has been drawn to the life of an Apostle being all glitter and glamorous. Meaning everything is a bowl of roses. I have suffered brokenness from Children, Siblings, Parents and Co Labors; major betrayal, Slander, lies and sabotage and the list go on. The Greatest feeling is knowing you are pleasing the heart of God and seeing the fruit of your Labor manifest in the lives of people is worth more than money, silver and gold.

The funny thing about it is, I became a used-up wash board to many of them, today it is as if I do not even exist to them. See this is the true life of one called to The Office of The Apostle, Used, Abused and Devalued by family, friends and The Religious Leaders. Jesus said, "A Prophet isn't received in his own town". You know why that is, because they can only see you in the natural, they cannot see who God has called you to be. They say, "That's just Valerie, what's so special about her." So, they will question your every move and motive.

Mark 6: 1-5 (King James Version)
And he went out from thence, and came into his own country; and his disciples followed him. 2And when the sabbath day was come, he began to teach in the synagogue: and many hearing him were astonished, saying, From whence hath this man these things? and what wisdom is this which is given unto him, that even such mighty works are wrought by his hands? 3Is not this the carpenter, the son of Mary, the brother of James, and Joses, and of Juda, and Simon? and are not his sisters here with us? And they were offended at him. 4But Jesus, said unto them, A prophet is not without honour, but in his own country, and among his own kin, and in his own house. 5And he could there do no mighty work, save that he laid his hands upon a few sick folk, and healed them.

When you are called to The Office of The Apostle, you will be hated by many, even your loved ones. Oftentimes, they will be jealous as well and you may frequently face betrayal just as Jesus did. Remember the story of Joseph and his brothers, Joseph told his dream to his brothers
50

and out of jealousy they plotted to kill Joseph. In the dream God said he would reign over his brothers. They could not phantom that, so Joseph's brothers plotted to kill and throw him into a pit. Joseph's destiny was already predestined by God and what they meant for evil, our Amazing God turned it around for his good (Ref. Genesis 37:1-36).

Everything that you will experience on this journey will eventually work in your favor: the good, the bad, and the ugly. God's purpose and plan is much bigger than the problems. One thing for sure the Promises of God remain Yes and Amen!
Every season is different, but they all serve as a major role in molding you as His Apostle.

Acts 9:15-16 (New King James Version)
15"But the Lord said to him, "Go, for he is a chosen vessel of Mine to bear My name before Gentiles, kings, and the children of Israel. 16For I will show him how many things he must suffer for My name's sake."

Galatians 6:9 (King James Version)
And let us not be weary in well doing: for in due season we shall reap, if we faint not.

God uses sculpting tools to help shape and mold us. Let me give you some examples for instance:

Beatitudes - Matthew 5:1-12 (New King James Version)
1 And seeing the multitudes, He went up on a mountain, and when He was seated His disciples came to Him. 2Then He opened His mouth and taught them, saying: 3Blessed are the poor in spirit, For theirs is the kingdom of heaven. 4Blessed are those who mourn, For they shall be comforted. 5Blessed are the meek, For they shall inherit the Earth. 6 Blessed are those who hunger and thirst for righteousness, For they shall be filled. 7Blessed are the merciful, For they shall obtain mercy. 8Blessed are the pure in heart, For they shall see God. 9 Blessed are the peacemakers, For they shall be called sons of God. 10Blessed are those who

**are persecuted for righteousness' sake, For theirs is the
kingdom of heaven. 11Blessed are you when they revile
and persecute you, and say all kinds of evil against you
falsely for My sake. 12 Rejoice and be exceedingly glad, for
great is your reward in heaven, for so they persecuted the
prophets who were before you.**

But, we must learn to Rest in God's Unfailing love and Provision for us
as King David did during tough times.

Psalm 23:1-6 (English Standard Version)
<u>A Psalm of David</u>

*The Lord is my shepherd; I shall not want. He makes me lie down in
green pastures. He leads me beside still waters. He restores my soul. He
leads me in paths of righteousness for his name's sake. Even though I
walk through the valley of the shadow of death, I will fear no evil, for you
are with me; your rod and your staff, they comfort me. You prepare a
table before me in the presence of my enemies; you anoint my head with
oil; my cup overflows…*

Matthew 10:22 (New King James Version)
**And you will be hated by all for My name's sake. But he who endures
to the end will be saved.**

The trials continued throughout our Spiritual Journey, but we are
Overcomers.

James 1:2-4 (King James Version)
**2My brethren, count it all joy when you fall into various trials,
3knowing that the testing of your faith produces patience. 4But
let patience have its perfect work, that you may be perfect and
complete, lacking nothing.**

If you are called to this scarce office of The Apostle, God truly must
call you because without His Grace and Affirmation you will not be
able to bear it.

Galatians 1:1 (New King James Version)
Paul, an apostle (not from men nor through man, but through Jesus Christ and God the Father who raised Him from the dead), ...

Overall, all Apostles are different. You must know your Spheres of Influence as an Apostle called and commissioned by God. Never mirror someone's anointing. Every person was created uniquely and is God's masterpiece. Never compare or compete with others. Embrace who you are, by doing so you will become more effective in your assignment.

As an Apostle, my strongest sphere of influence is with The Broken, Bruise and Wounded, those that were left for dead. Healing and deliverance are the Core of my ministry. Not only has God called me to perform miracles, signs and wonders, but He has graced me to teach others how to walk in their ministry of Healing and Deliverance. One of the graces on the lives of an Apostle is they love to teach and impart into others.

Romans 1:11 (King James Version)
For I long to see you, that I may impart unto you some spiritual gift, to the end ye may be established; ...

Chapter Five

Supernatural Encounters

I will now share some of my most amazing encounters. One was when I went to heaven in an outer body experience like Paul. I really do not know whether I was in my body or out of it. In 2010 we were coming to a close in a worship service at my local church which was referred to by many as the Upper Room, well, the power of The Holy Spirit came in like a rushing mighty wind and I had an out of body, I experience where I entered into heaven. "My God the experience was like nothing you've ever imagined," all I can remember is seeing this water that was so clear that you could see straight through it. The water had no end, the trees were so beautiful, I mean breathtaking, everything was so serene. The air was so pure and fresh, when I came to, I could not hardly breathe because of the change in the air. It was so amazing, and I knew He had shown me a glimpse. Later it was confirmed by one of my Co-labors that was standing by. He said, "You left us, and God showed you a glimpse of heaven."

My next Supernatural encounter was in prayer. I entered a place of prayer that I had never entered before. My room had changed and suddenly it was if God's Glory was filling the entire room. I could not stop praying in the spirit, it got more and more intense. I felt water pouring from my head, then I felt this tap on my head, which was not forceful it was light. The Holy Spirit said, "Look down on the floor!" I did as I was told, and there was a beautiful stone as a black onyx, full of a mixture of other colors, one of the most beautiful stones I had ever seen. I was overjoyed at first. I thought I was crazy, but I shared it with a friend who is in ministry as well and she said, "Oh my Goodness you received one of your jewels!" I looked the stone up and sure enough, it is a biblical stone.

I have experienced several miracles long before I even knew that I was an Apostle. I was a novice and I remember my Pastor asking me to pray for a Female Pastor from New York and I was thinking, "why am I praying for a Pastor who am I?" Being obedient I did as I was told, and low and behold God healed the Pastor instantly. The doctors confirmed what I had seen, God healing her. My Pastor was so elated when the confirmation came in. I did not have a clear understanding at that time, but God was training me up.

In 2020, I experienced a man being healed on a Zoom meeting I was facilitating, God showed me this man blood was off and he was experiencing stroke-like symptoms online. Holy Spirit had me to take authority over the root of it and immediately the man was overjoyed of his healing. I told him to go to the doctors to get it confirmed and they said they could no longer find the blood clot anymore!

The God that we serve does miracles and He is given those who believe in Him that same authority over sickness and disease, Apostles have been given a Supernatural Grace to walk-in Tangible miracles signs and wonders, but you must have the faith to understand that we have been given supernatural ability and power through The Holy Spirit to walk the Earth just as Jesus Christ walked the Earth exemplify miracles everywhere he went. Casting out Devils and Healing all manner of sickness and disease. Restoring the sight to the blind, causing the lame to get up and walk and we have been given this same power and we must begin to execute it in the Earth realm especially those that have a calling to be Apostles and Believers.

would consider myself a Praying Apostle. Everything I have established and birthed is out of prayer and intercession my passion is prayer. I have experienced miracles being performed through the power of prayer. I have seen miraculous signs and wonders. I believe you must be very disciplined in prayer and committed to a life of prayer and fasting.

God uses me in prayer to minister healing to the broken-hearted; and deliverance to those that are being held captives by the enemy devices. One of my strongest gifts are discerning of spirits and word knowledge when praying for someone to be delivered and healed these gifts reveal the root of the issue.

Every Apostle is unique and peculiar and their own right. I know I am peculiar, not strange or spooky but yes peculiar. My life is dedicated to The Lord and the yielding and guiding of the Holy Spirit. I have learned to weather the storms, stand firm and remain unmovable steadfast and always abounding in the work of The Lord know my labors not in vain. I do not fit Him into my world but I Live in Him he is my world! Though this Apostolic Charge has been rough at times through the years I have seen the evidence of His Grace upon the Call.

I am embracing this place that is very unpredictable but as long as I know He's all in it with me I know for sure I can continue on with great strength and power because He cares so much for me.
fear not, for I am with you; be not dismayed, for I am your God; I will strengthen you, I will help you, I will uphold you with my righteous right hand (Isaiah 41:10).

God will always cover and protect us on our journeys never loss trust in God because He always comes through. When you pass through the waters, I will be with you; and through the rivers, they shall not overwhelm you; when you walk through fire you shall not be burned, and the flame shall not consume you (Isaiah 43:2).

I have discovered on this Apostolic Journey the most important lesson is yielding to The Power of The Holy Spirit always obeying The Lord, remaining humble and operating out of His love, remembering it is not about you. You are a Living Sacrifice. Your life is not your own anymore you have been bought with a price which was purchased with His Blood.

Romans 12:1-2 (King James Version)
12 I beseech you therefore, brethren, by the mercies of God, that

you present your bodies a living sacrifice, holy, acceptable to God, which is your reasonable service. 2And do not be conformed to this world, but be transformed by the renewing of your mind, that you may prove what is that good and acceptable and perfect will of God.

Never concentrate on the pain, the purpose will out way the pain, the pain is the process to produce the purpose. Processes are necessary God allows them, they help to prune mold shape and perfect our fruit. We cannot produce more fruit without the pruning.

John 15:1-8 (New International Version)
15 I am the true vine, and my Father is the gardener. 2He cuts off every branch in me that bears no fruit, while every branch that does bear fruit he prunes[a] so that it will be even more fruitful. 3You are already clean because of the word I have spoken to you. 4Remain in me, as I also remain in you. No branch can bear fruit by itself; it must remain in the vine. Neither can you bear fruit unless you remain in me. 5"I am the vine; you are the branches. If you remain in me and I in you, you will bear much fruit; apart from me you can do nothing. 6If you do not remain in me, you are like a branch that is thrown away and withers; such branches are picked up, thrown into the fire and burned. 7If you remain in me and my words remain in you, ask whatever you wish, and it will be done for you. 8This is to my Father's glory, that you bear much fruit, showing yourselves to be my disciples. Apostle Paul suffered, He went to prison for the sake of the gospel what is persecuted light on defamed and hated for preaching the gospel.

As I prepare to end, let us see the examples of The Apostles in The Bible and how each of them had a Diversity in their function but the same Spirit working in them all. I will use Apostle Paul, Apostle Peter and Apostle James.

1 Corinthians 12:4-11 (New International Version)
4There are different kinds of gifts, but the same Spirit distributes them. 5There are different kinds of service, but the same Lord. 6There are different kinds of working, but in all of them and in everyone it

is the same God at work. 7Now to each one the manifestation of the Spirit is given for the common good. 8To one there is given through the Spirit a message of wisdom, to another a message of knowledge by means of the same Spirit, 9to another faith by the same Spirit, to another gifts of healing by that one Spirit, 10to another miraculous powers, to another prophecy, to another distinguishing between spirits, to another speaking in different kinds of tongues, and to still another the interpretation of tongues. 11All these are the work of one and the same Spirit, and he distributes them to each one, just as he determines.

More than anything I want you to be able to see that it is only God that calls Apostles and graces them for what He has predestined them for. For example, Apostle Paul was called to The Gentiles, He preached with such boldness proclaiming that Jesus is The Son of God!

Acts 9:20–22 (English Standard Version)
20And immediately he proclaimed Jesus in the synagogues, saying, "He is the Son of God." 21 And all who heard him were amazed and said, "Is not this the man who made havoc in Jerusalem of those who called upon this name? And has he not come here for this purpose, to bring …to bring them bound before the chief priests?" 22But Saul increased all the more in strength and confounded the Jews who lived in Damascus by proving that Jesus was the Christ.

<u>Saul Escapes from Damascus</u>
Acts 9:23–31 (English Standard Version)
23When many days had passed, the Jews1 plotted to kill him, 24but their plot became known to Saul. They were watching the gates day and night in order to kill him, 25but his disciples took him by night and let him down through an opening in the wall, lowering him in a basket.

<u>Saul in Jerusalem</u>
26And when he had come to Jerusalem, he attempted to join the disciples. And they were all afraid of him, for they did not believe that he was a disciple. 27But Barnabas took him and brought him to the apostles and declared to them how on the road he had seen the Lord, who spoke to him, and

how at Damascus he had preached boldly in the name of Jesus. 28So he went in and out among them at Jerusalem, preaching boldly in the name of the Lord. 29And he spoke and disputed against the Hellenists. But they were seeking to kill him. 30And when the brothers learned this, they brought him down to Caesarea and sent him off to Tarsus. 31So the church throughout all Judea and Galilee and Samaria had peace and was being built up. And walking in the fear of the Lord and in the comfort of the Holy Spirit, it multiplied.

Apostle Paul was also a Scribe who penned many New Testament Books, which I've listed here:

- *Galatians (AD 47)*
- *1 and 2 Thessalonians (AD 49—51)*
- *1 and 2 Corinthians and Romans (AD 52—56)*
- *Ephesians, Philemon, Colossians, and Philippians (AD 60—62, during Paul's first Roman imprisonment)*
- *1 Timothy and Titus (AD 62)*
- *2 Timothy (AD 63—64, during Paul's second Roman imprisonment)*

He also was a planter of many churches and traveled many mission trips. Apostle Paul's mission and passion was overall to fulfill that purpose and The Perfect Will of God with The Empowering of The Holy Spirit. Apostle said that.

Philippians 4:13 (New King James Version)
I can do all things through Christ who strengthens me. Overall Apostle Paul understood Christ is the reason he was able to function as The Apostle God had called him to be.

Zachariah 4:6 (Amplified Version)
Then he said to me, "This [continuous supply of oil] is the word of the Lord to Zerubbabel [prince of Judah], saying, 'Not by might, nor by power, but by My Spirit [of whom the oil is a symbol],' says the Lord of hosts.

Apostle Peter, an Apostle to The Jews, full of Holy Ghost Power, preached and the power of His preaching radically changed many lives, The Bible records that Peter's shadow was anointed. We see in

Acts 5:15 (Amplified Version) that it describes the accounts of Peter healing many sick people and casting out many demons in the name of Jesus Christ.

Acts 5:15-16 (Amplified Version)
15to such an extent that they even carried their sick out into the streets and put them on cots and sleeping pads, so that when Peter came by at least his shadow might fall on one of them [with healing power]. 16And the people from the towns in the vicinity of Jerusalem were coming together, bringing the sick and those who were tormented by unclean spirits, and they were all being healed.

The same Ascension Gifts, but diversities in their Spheres of Influence and remember, by the same Spirit!

There are NO duplicates in the eyes of God only Designer's Originals and being made in the Image of God is a high honor and privilege -- no one greater to Image, but God!! As I end, I want to declare some things over your lives.

Job 22:28 (Amplified Version)
You will also decide and decree a thing, and it will be established for you; And the light [of God's favor] will shine upon your ways.

****

Let me make this declaration over your life as you read this book. "I am fearfully and wonderfully made, I was created with greatness and I have purpose, my purpose is great, and I will accomplish everything God created me for. I am more than a conqueror in Christ Jesus Our Lord! I will not be defeated; I will not die, but I will rise up and continue to declare the works of The Lord! I am chosen, hand selected and pre-qualified to walk out my purpose and my destiny I am who God says I am, I am Chosen! No weapons that attempt to form against me will be able to prosper, because He is my strong tower and my fortress, and I put all my trust in Him alone!"

The True Life of an Apostle

God knows what we can bear because He created us for His use and Graced us for our predestined journey. I pray that someone who may be reading this will be blessed. Your life will be changed, and you will have a greater understanding of The life of an Apostle. May God's plans and purpose for your life be fulfilled and prosperous in Jesus' name.

Signed,
God's Servant for Life
Apostle Dr. Valerie Jackson

Questions

(The answers are found in the Chapters of this Book)

1. Ask yourself what are some of the characteristics that I have equal to the calling of an Apostle

2. Who calls Apostles?

3. Is this calling gender restricted?

4. How does God Call Apostles?

5. Do all Apostles plant churches?

6. Do all Apostles Pastor?

7. How important is it to be validated by other Apostles, is this biblical?

8. Do Apostles Suffer greatly?

9. Are Apostles Commissioned or Ordained? What defines Authentic Apostles from an Imposter?

10. Should Every Apostle function in all the Ascension Gifts listed in Ephesians 4:11?

11.   Do you have to attend Seminary and School of Divinity to be an Apostle?

12.   Why is it important for Apostles to work closely with Prophets?

Ephesians 4:11-13 (Amplified Version)
11And [His gifts to the church were varied and] He Himself appointed some as apostles [special messengers, representatives], some as prophets [who speak a new message from God to the people], some as evangelists [who spread the good news of salvation], and some as pastors and teachers [to shepherd and guide and instruct], 12[and He did this] to fully equip and perfect the saints (God's people) for works of service, to build up the body of Christ [the church]; 13until we all reach oneness in the faith and in the knowledge of the Son of God, [growing spiritually] to become a mature believer, reaching to the measure of the fullness of Christ [manifesting His spiritual completeness and exercising our spiritual gifts in unity].

Notes

Definitions

Apostles: Special Messengers sent by God, Sent Ones, Ambassadors for Christ

Prophets: They guide, they are Spokesmen for God that foretell, forthtell and release the mind of God.

Evangelists: Soul winners that witness & Preach the death, burial and resurrection of Christ (Gatherers)

Teachers: Teach and instruct the word of God (Logos) to The Body by rightly dividing and studying to show themselves approved unto God.

Pastors: Guard, protect, feed the word of God; (Logos & Rhema) to the flock God Entrusted to them.

Now concerning spiritual gifts, brethren, I do not want you to be uninformed" (1 Corinthians 12:1 – Revised Standard Version).

The Gifts of the Holy Spirit
1 Corinthians 12:4, 7-11
Defining the word "gift"
Defined: The Nine Gifts of The Spirit
Greek word charisma khar'-is-mah (Strong's Greek Number 5486)

Charisma khar'-is-mah is grace made definite, specific, effective, available in a certain form or operation in the life of a believer.

Gifts of Revelation:
1) The Word of Wisdom:
   A supernatural revelation, or insight into the divine will and purpose, often given by the Spirit to solve perplexing problems and situations.

2) The Word of Knowledge:
   The Word of Knowledge is a supernatural revelation of Divine knowledge or insight in the Divine mind, will or plan, to know things that could not be known of oneself.

3) Discerning of Spirits:
   This is a supernatural revelation or insight into the realm of spirits to detect their presence and plans.

Gifts of Inspiration
4) Prophecy:
   Prophecy is the supernatural utterance in the native tongue. It is a miracle of divine utterance, not conceived by human thought or reasoning. It includes speaking unto men to edification, exhortation, and comfort.

5) Divers Kinds of Tongues:
   The supernatural utterance in other languages that are not known to the speaker.

6) The Interpretation of Tongues:
   The supernatural ability to interpret in the native tongue what is uttered in other languages not known by the one who interprets by the Spirit.

Gifts of Power
7) The Gift of Faith:
   This is a supernatural ability to believe God without human doubt, unbelief, and reasonings.

8) The Gift of Healing:
The healing of all manner of sickness by supernatural power, without human aid or medicine.

9) The Working of Miracles:
Is supernatural power to intervene in the ordinary course of nature and to counteract natural laws if necessary.

The word spirit: The word spirit is rendered as רוּחַ (ruach) in Hebrew-language parts of the Old Testament. In its Aramaic parts, the term is rûach. The Greek translation of the Old Testament, the Septuagint, translates the word as πνεῦμα (pneuma – "breath").

The Holy Spirit: The third person of The Godhead, The Spirit of God, Paraclete (Greek: παράκλητος, Latin: paracletus) means advocate or helper. ... In Christianity, the term "paraclete" most commonly refers to the Holy Spirit.

References

King James, Amplified and New and Living Bibles
Gateway, Biblia and Biblical Dictionary
Webster Online Dictionary
Google Search
King James Biblical Online Dictionary
Hebrew and Greek Concise
Wikipedia (Online)

APOSTLE DR. VALERIE JACKSON is a Visionary and an End Time Handmaiden of the Lord; one whom God has called out for such a time as this to unequivocally declare the Word of Truth with authority and power. As a yielded vessel, she has been anointed and equipped to carry out this mandate by bringing reformation and restoration to the Body of Christ under an apostolic and prophetic mantle. She has been laboring to bring sound truth and deliverance to the Body of Christ at large through her humility and obedience to Christ as the Lord allows her to minister during leadership conferences, revivals, and deliverance services. She is the Co-Author of two published books, He Still Sees and The Breaking to Brilliant Pastor's Edition's on Healing from Grief.

Apostle Dr. Valerie has a passion and love for people from all walks of life. As a young girl, she told her mom she wanted to help take care of people and make them happy. Little did she know that God had a plan and purpose that included doing that and more. Early in her life, she established a women's group called "Oasis." This group was geared to help women get off the streets, learn life skills, and character development. She spent hours mentoring and empowering women who were on the verge of giving up on life due to traumatic circumstances such as physical and mental abuse, molestation and rape. Apostle Valerie never made them feel like victims and she taught them that their lives were not over because of these horrific events; she told them God wanted to make them whole. After escaping a 10-year abusive relationship, this became her passion. She knew if God did it for her, He will do for them as well because of His love for us! She desired to see lives forever changed and as a result of this group, many of these women have become successful in life. Many are business owners; many have acquired full-time employment; and some serve as ordained ministers.

Apostle Dr. Valerie desires to see men and women of God free and restored to fulfill their God given purpose. As a result of this passion, she provides wisdom and counseling to those who are in need. She also counsels' leaders from different churches who experience pitfalls while in ministry. She mentors many, not for money or any selfish motives, but she believes everyone deserves a second chance.

In 2008, Apostle Valerie established an International Prayer Ministry which traveled the East Coast and within the Bahamas. She one day she hopes it will travel to Haiti. While ministering in Florida, she connected with a Haitian Community and began a weekly Bible Study conference call which gave them access to the Word of God from the luxury of their homes. She facilitated weekly conference prayer and Bible study calls which resulted in many souls receiving salvation during these calls. Today, the prayer line has grown in numbers and many prayers have been answered because of the consistent prayer that continues each day. The torch for facilitating the prayer line has been passed to her mentees who are just a passionate as she was upon inception.

Apostle Dr. Valerie Jackson is the Founder and Presiding Prelate of Made In His Image International Ministries, Inc., where she serves alongside her husband, Pastor Lynn Jackson, and best friend of 22 years. Together, they have six children and five grandchildren and many spiritual children in the Kingdom of God.

Apostle Jackson is also the founder of The Wells of Living Water Prophetic International Prayer Ministry, The School of the Flow of the Holy Spirit, and the Apostolic Council to Servants (ACTS). ACTS is an apostolic mentoring and spiritual covering ministry for senior leaders, churches and entrepreneurs that need spiritual guidance and counsel. In 2005, Apostle Jackson was ordained and affirmed Pastor under the leadership of Apostle Antonio Briggs of Radical Apostolic Power International Ministries in Washington, D.C., where she served as an ordained minister and intercessor until transitioning.

In 2008, Apostle Jackson was installed Pastor of Made In His Image Ministries under the leadership of Apostle Edward Ramsey and co-leadership of Apostle Curtis Schultz of Agape Christian Center in Baltimore, MD and Pathfinders Ministries in Savage, MD. Her ministry training includes: The School of Prophets, Old and New Testament Studies, Warfare and Intercessory Prayer Training, Crises Counseling, Substance and Alcohol Abuse Counseling, HIV & AIDS, and Life Skills Counseling. Apostle Jackson has many prolific teachers in the Gospel that have nurtured and imparted much wisdom and knowledge into grooming her for her Apostolic Charge. Today, she remains in Covenant Relationship with all her teachers. Apostle Valerie is submitted and accountable to her spiritual covering Apostle James H. Kithcart of Mountain Top International Ministries in Texas.

In April of 2014, Apostle Valerie Jackson was elevated and consecrated to the Office of Apostle. In 2020 Apostle Valerie completed her Biblical Studies in Pastoral Counseling as well as received an Honorary Doctorate in Divinity from Elbon Solution College of Ministries in Apple Valley, CA and earned a Her greatest assignment in the Kingdom of God as one of an Ardent Worshiper. She believes that true worship becomes a lifestyle as you obey and commit yourself to the perfect will of God. Through her worship, she experiences the Glory of God to perform miracles, signs, and wonders!

For more information, please contact Pastor Faye Thomas by email at pastorfaye24@gmail.com or by phone at (301) 848-0839.

Spiritual Gifts:
I am a Prophetic Apostle. I am intuitive and a spontaneous leader who has the ability to think quickly with words of wisdom from the Lord. Prophetic Apostles are great visionaries and dreamers and think ahead of the curve and have a great gift of exhortation and/or preaching

extemporaneously. With this great gift of motivation, a prophetic apostle is able to attract many leaders into their Spheres of Influence.

Additional Gifting(s):
• Governmental Prophet
• Apostolic Teacher
• Pastor
• Word of Knowledge
• Word of Wisdom
• Gift of Healing
• Discerning of Spirits
• Divers Tongues
• Gift of Leadership
• Gift of Administration

Training:
2009-2010 – Pathfinder Ministries, Savage MM
Facilitator, Apostle Curtis Schultz
• School of the Prophets
• Old and New Testament

2008-2009
Facilitator, Prophet LeRon Atkins
• How to Properly Exegesis
• The Scriptures/The Study of Christology
• Angels and Demons

2006-2007 – APRA, District of Columbia Government
Facilitator, Dr. Mike Nettles
• Substance and Alcohol Abuse Counseling, Life Skills, Crisis Intervention, HIV Support and Advocacy

2004-2005 – Intro to Hermeneutics
Facilitator, Apostle Dr. Earnest Quick

www.ingramcontent.com/pod-product-compliance
Lightning Source LLC
LaVergne TN
LVHW010316070426
835513LV00021B/2407